Published By Adam Gilbin

@ Roger Watt

Chat Gpt: A Beginner's Guide to Chatgpt-assisted

Programmin Chat Gpt and Prompt Engineering

Mastery for Professionals

All Right RESERVED

ISBN 978-87-94477-74-1

TABLE OF CONTENTS

Chapter 1 1

What Is Chat Gpt? 1

Chapter 2 3

Evolution And Development Of Chat Gpt Models 3

Chapter 3 14

Creating Viral Video Content With Chat Gpt 14

Chapter 4 19

Understanding Chatgpt And The Ai Landscape 19

Chapter 5 24

What Is Chatgpt And How Does It Work? 24

Chapter 6 29

Chatgpt Limitations And Capabilities 29

Chapter 7 34

Ethical And Legal Considerations 34

Chapter 8 38

The Science And Art Of Prompting 38

Chapter 9 44

Fundamentals Of Natural Language Processing And Chatbots 44

Chapter 10 54

Content Creation Services Using Chat Gpt 54

Chapter 11 68

Unleashing The Power Of Chatgpt 68

Chapter 12 72

The Problem With Prompts 72

Chapter 13 83

The Business Of Chat Gpt 83

Chapter 14 88

The Ethical Considerations Of Chatgpt 88

Chapter 15 92

The Digital Goldmine: Understanding Chatgpt's Earning Potential 92

Monetizing Conversations: *Turning Dialogue Into Dollars* 99

Chapter 16 114

The Chatgpt Revolution: Your Key To Unlocking A World Of Opportunities.. 114

Chapter 17 123

Getting Started With Chatgpt: The Life-Changing Opportunity You Can't Miss 123

Chapter 1

What is Chat GPT?

Chat GPT, or Chat Generative Pre trained Transformer, is a type of artificial intelligence model developed by OpenAI. It is specifically designed for generating human-like text and engaging in conversations. Chat GPT models are trained on a vast amount of text data from the internet, allowing **them to understand and generate text in a way that mimics human language and conversation.**
These models have the ability to respond coherently to text inputs, making them suitable for chatbots, virtual assistants, content

generation, and various natural language processing tasks. Chat GPT models are used in a wide range of applications, including customer support chatbots, content creation, language translation, and more. They have gained popularity due to their versatility and the ability to automate and improve text-based communication.

For example, if you input a question or statement, a Chat GPT model can generate a response that is contextually relevant and appears as if it were written by a human, making it a valuable tool for various text-based application

Chapter 2

Evolution and Development of Chat GPT Models

The growth and progress of AI language models designed for conversation. In summary:

Chat GPT models have come a long way from early,

rule-based chatbots.

GPT-2 was a significant advancement in generating

coherent text.

GPT-3 marked a giant leap in AI language modeling.

Chat GPT models emerged as specialized, contextaware chatbot models.

Continuous research and development drive improvements in these models, ensuring a promising
future in conversation AI.

This ebook stands apart from others by focusing specifically on the needs of teachers who aspire to write a book. It offers a streamlined approach that enables educators to effectively share their expertise in their area of education within a remarkably short timeframe.

Just as a rock-climbing partner provides guidance, encouragement, and practical tips to overcome challenges, Chat GPT empowers you to conquer the hurdles of writing. It offers a multitude of benefits that make it an indispensable asset for educators:

Expertise on Tap: Chat GPT acts as a vast repository of information, akin to a trusty guide well-versed in various educational topics. It can provide insights, facts, and explanations to enhance the depth and accuracy of your content.

Creative Spark: Like an adventurous climbing partner who inspires you to explore new routes, Chat GPT ignites your creativity. It generates fresh ideas, unique perspectives, and innovative approaches that breathe life into your writing, making it engaging and captivating for your students.

Time Efficiency: Just as a skilled partner helps you navigate the rock face efficiently, Chat GPT accelerates your writing process. It assists in drafting content, saving you precious time and energy. With its prompt-based assistance, you can swiftly overcome writer's block and effortlessly organize your thoughts.

Language Mastery: A proficient climbing partner understands the nuances of climbing techniques and communicates them effectively. Similarly, Chat GPT comprehends language intricacies, ensuring your content is articulate, coherent, and tailored to your intended audience.

Adaptability and Flexibility: Like an adaptable climbing partner who adjusts to various terrains, Chat GPT is versatile in addressing diverse educational needs. Whether you're creating lesson plans, developing teaching materials, or crafting engaging assessments, it adapts to your requirements, providing valuable assistance every step of the way.

Continuous Learning: Just as climbing partners continually expand their knowledge and skills, Chat GPT evolves through continuous learning. It stays updated with the latest educational trends, research, and best practices, ensuring you have access to cutting-edge information.

Collaboration: A collaborative climbing partner fosters teamwork and shares the joy of achievement. Similarly, Chat GPT enables collaboration by facilitating seamless communication between educators, allowing you to exchange ideas, provide feedback, and collectively improve the quality of educational content.

In essence, Chat GPT is your ultimate rock-climbing partner, propelling you to new heights in the realm of content creation. It combines expertise, creativity, efficiency, language mastery, adaptability, continuous learning, and collaboration—all essential factors that make it an indispensable ally for educators. You will witness how Chat GPT transforms your content creation process, making your educational materials rock-solid and captivating for your students.

Now, Let's get this party started. The following information will provide you with clear steps on how to log onto Chat GPT AI Open. Get your computer and do it!

Accessing Chat GPT AI Open

Open a web browser on your computer or mobile device. I use google chrome.
Go to the OpenAI website (
Look for the "Chat GPT AI Open" section and click on the provided link.

Familiarizing Yourself with Chat GPT AI Open

Once you're on the Chat GPT AI Open page, take a moment to read the instructions and get an overview of how it works.
Familiarize yourself with the various input and output options available to interact with the Chat GPT.

Generating Prompts (Prompts are provided in each chapter)

Before you start writing your eBook, it's important to generate suitable prompts to guide the AI.

Begin by brainstorming ideas and themes for your eBook. Consider your passions, interests, and knowledge.

Once you have a clear idea, formulate a concise prompt that will help the AI understand the direction you want to take.

Example: "Write a chapter about the importance of environmental conservation and its impact on future generations."

Interacting with Chat GPT AI Open

On the Chat GPT AI Open page, locate the input box labeled "User" or "You."

Type in a brief introduction to your eBook project and your first prompt.

To ensure effective prompts, it is crucial to maintain clarity, specificity, and a singular focus on each topic or idea. When engaging Chat GPT, provide it with well-defined tasks (verbs) and precise parameters (such as length, list, or numbers), allowing it to respond accordingly. In the context of Bloom's Taxonomy, utilizing detailed action verbs aligned with each level of cognitive skill enhances the quality of prompts. I will add a Bonus Prompt Page with Bloom's Terms at the end of this ebook.

Experiment with different prompts and see how the AI responds. If you need more guidance or ideas, you can continue the conversation with the AI.

Writing an eBook with Prompts

Use Chat GPT and the prompts in the following chapters as a starting point for your eBook content.

Analyze the generated text and extract relevant information or ideas.

Craft your own sentences and paragraphs based on the ChatGPT's response, using your unique writing style and voice.

Incorporate your own research and knowledge to enhance the quality and accuracy of your eBook.

Continue the process by providing new prompts and using the AI's responses to guide your writing.

Editing and Refining Your eBook

After completing the initial draft of your eBook, it is essential to take a deliberate pause and approach it with a fresh perspective. Allow yourself a minimum of 24 hours before revisiting your work. Learning from my own past experiences, rushing the publication process can result in numerous corrections with publishers, causing significant inconveniences and setbacks. Read through your eBook, ensuring the content flows smoothly and aligns with your intended message.

Make necessary revisions, add additional information or anecdotes, and remove any irrelevant or redundant sections.

Edit for grammar, spelling, punctuation, and overall clarity.

Consider seeking feedback from trusted individuals such as teachers, friends, or family members to further improve your eBook.

Chapter 3

Creating Viral Video Content with Chat GPT

ChatGPT is not only a powerful tool for creating written content, but it can also be used to generate video scripts that can be used to create viral videos. In this chapter, we'll discuss how to use ChatGPT to create video scripts, and how to monetize that video content through advertising and sponsorships.

Scriptwriting with ChatGPT

The first step in creating viral video content with ChatGPT is to generate a script. This can be done by providing the model with a general topic and asking it to generate a script that is optimized for that topic. For example, if you want to create a viral video about "dog grooming," you could provide the model with that topic and ask it to generate a script that is optimized for that topic. It's important to keep in mind that the script generated by ChatGPT is not final, and it is important to edit, proofread and fact-check the script before filming. ChatGPT can be used as a tool to generate ideas, but a human touch is always needed to make it better and more captivating.

When generating a script, it's important to keep in mind the audience and the tone that you want to convey. ChatGPT can generate scripts for different types of videos such as comedic, educational, or informative videos. By providing the model with specific examples of the type of script you want to generate, ChatGPT can generate a script that is tailored to your needs.

Monetizing Video Content Through Advertising and Sponsorships

Once you have a script, you can use it to create a video that can be monetized through advertising and sponsorships. Advertising and sponsorships are two of the most common ways to monetize video content. Advertising is when a business pays you to include their product or service in your video. Sponsorships are when a business pays you to create a video that promotes their product or service.

To monetize your video content through advertising, you can use platforms like YouTube, which allows you to include ads in your videos. You can also use platforms like Facebook, Instagram, and TikTok, which also have advertising options. Additionally, you can monetize your video content through sponsorships. This can be done by reaching out to businesses in your niche and pitching them your video content. You can also use platforms like

TikTok, which has a Creator Fund program, to monetize your videos.

It's important to keep in mind that in order to monetize your video content through advertising and sponsorships, you need to have a significant following and engagement. The more views and engagement your videos have, the more valuable they will be to businesses looking to advertise or sponsor content.

Real-world Examples of Viral Videos Generated with ChatGPT

While the usage of ChatGPT for scriptwriting is a new and emerging trend, there are not many real-world examples of viral videos generated with ChatGPT yet. However, it's important to note that ChatGPT is a powerful tool for generating text, and it can be used to generate scripts for any type of video.

In conclusion, ChatGPT can be a powerful tool for creating viral video content. By using ChatGPT to generate scripts, you can create videos that are highly engaging and relevant to your target audience. Additionally, by monetizing your video content through advertising and sponsorships, you can generate significant revenue. However, it's important to keep in mind that ChatGPT is a tool, and a human touch is always needed to make a video truly captivating.

Chapter 4

Understanding ChatGPT and the AI landscape

History of AI in text generation

Understanding the history of artificial intelligence (AI) in text generation is a valuable first step in understanding where we are now and the way forward. This exploration takes us back to the early stages of computing, where the very idea that a machine could "think" or even "write" was considered the stuff of science fiction. With technological advances and improvements in algorithms, today we have practical applications of AI in a variety of fields, including text generation.

Early approaches to natural language processing (NLP) in the 1950s and 1960s were predominantly rule-based models. These models required experts to manually encode grammar and syntax rules to interpret or generate text. This resulted in very limited systems that were not very adaptable and required constant maintenance to evolve.

Over time, the focus shifted to statistical models and, later, to machine learning models. These models allow machines to "learn" from data rather than relying on predefined rules. A key moment in this evolution was the emergence of the backpropagation algorithm in the 1980s, which made neural networks viable for complex tasks, including NLP.

Entering the 21st century, the adoption of deep learning models marked a sea change in AI performance in a variety of applications. Language models such as Word2Vec and GloVe enabled better handling of semantics and syntax by creating vector representations of words in a multidimensional space. These models led to more sophisticated algorithms that could interpret the structure and meaning of text more effectively.

An important milestone was the development of Transformers, first presented in the paper "Attention Is All You Need" in 2017. This new type of neural network architecture led to a new generation of more effective and versatile language models. Transformers stand out for their ability to handle long-distance relationships within text and for their training efficiency.

The birth of GPT (Generative Pre-trained Transformer) was another game-changing breakthrough. Developed by OpenAI, GPT-2 proved to be extremely capable of generating coherent and contextually relevant text. Its successor, GPT-3, has pushed the boundaries even further, reaching levels that can sometimes make it difficult to distinguish between human-generated text and machine-generated text. This is where we are today, with ChatGPT being a specialized version of GPT-4 designed for conversations and, as we will see in the next chapters, to assist us in content generation.

It is essential to point out that, although the capabilities of these models are amazing, they also have their limitations. They face problems such as the generation of false information, the lack of real understanding of the world and certain ethical considerations that are still being discussed in the scientific and ethical community.

As we look at this historical journey, we can appreciate how quickly technology has advanced and how it has opened new doors in the generation of text. We can also see that the practical applications of these advances are rapidly changing the way we interact with information, create content and communicate.

This advance in AI for text generation has become a valuable resource for writers, editors and content creators. It offers possibilities to speed up the writing process, generate ideas and even monetize content in previously unimaginable ways.

While the future remains uncertain, the past and present offer us an interesting perspective on the potential of this technology. As we move forward, we are likely to see more innovations and improvements that will make AI-assisted text generation an increasingly important part of our lives. With this foundation, we are better prepared to understand the following chapters, which will guide us on how to use these tools effectively to write books and monetize them in the online environment.

Chapter 5

What is ChatGPT and how does it work?

ChatGPT, or Generative Pre-trained Transformer, is a generative language model developed by OpenAI. It is one of the most advanced models of its kind and is based on the Transformer architecture, which is also used in other areas of artificial intelligence (AI), such as computer vision and natural language processing. But what does it all really mean and how does it translate into a useful tool for writing books?

First, we will analyze the basic structure of a generative language model. These models are essentially machine learning algorithms trained on a large volume of textual data. During this training, the model learns to recognize patterns in the text, such as grammar, context, style, and more. Once sufficiently trained, the model can generate text that is coherent, contextually relevant, and, in many cases, indistinguishable from text written by a human.

The Transformer architecture is the technical foundation of ChatGPT. This architecture consists of what are known as "attention" layers, which allow the model to make complex connections between different words and phrases in a text stream. Attention" helps the model understand the context in which certain words and phrases are used, allowing it to generate more coherent and contextually appropriate responses. In short, it gives the model a kind of temporal "memory" that it uses to produce high-quality text.

So how does ChatGPT work in practice? Typically, you will interact with ChatGPT through an online interface or an API (Application Programming Interface). To generate text, you give the model a "hint" or "propmpt", which is a small amount of text that serves as input to generate a more detailed response. For example, if you are writing a book about gardening, you might provide a prompt such as "Explain how to plant tomatoes". ChatGPT would take this prompt and generate a detailed response, which could include everything from soil selection and planting time, to care to be taken to ensure a successful harvest.

One of the most striking advantages of using ChatGPT for writing is the speed at which you can generate content. While the quality of the text generated may vary and generally requires some form of editing afterwards, the ability to produce large volumes of text in a short period of time is unparalleled. This is especially useful for writers looking to maximize their productivity, or for those facing tight deadlines.

That said, it is important to note that ChatGPT is not without its limitations. For one thing, while it is very good at maintaining consistency over small portions of text, it can struggle with longer texts.

This is because the model has a limited "attention window", meaning that it can only consider a certain amount of previous words when generating new output. This limitation can lead to responses that are grammatically correct but lack broader context or overall coherence.

In addition, ChatGPT cannot verify facts, cite sources, or perform tasks that require a deep or specialized understanding of the subject matter. For example, if you are writing an academic book that requires detailed bibliographic references and rigorous methodology, ChatGPT would not be able to handle these tasks autonomously. While it can generate text that sounds accurate and well-informed, it is the human writer's responsibility to verify the accuracy and reliability of the information.

Last but not least, there is always the risk of generating text that has already been published by others, given that the model has been trained on a large corpus of data that includes a wide range of publicly available sources. This implies the need to employ plagiarism detection tools and to carry out a thorough review to ensure that the generated content is unique.

Chapter 6

ChatGPT limitations and capabilities

Understanding ChatGPT's limitations and capabilities is a fundamental starting point if you have in mind to write a book with its help. A thorough understanding of what this technology can and cannot do will not only enrich the quality of your work, but also improve the efficiency of the writing process.

Let's start with the capabilities of ChatGPT. Broadly speaking, this language model is designed to generate text that resembles human language. Its strength lies in creating grammatically correct sentences, generating coherent dialogue and, in certain cases, presenting information in a logical and structured manner. It can produce content in a variety of styles and tones, making it highly adaptable to different genres of writing. In addition, you have the ability to continue and maintain a thematic thread throughout a text, although this may vary depending on the size of the text and the details provided for its generation.

If you need content in large volumes, ChatGPT can be a valuable resource. The speed of text generation is noticeably faster compared to an average human being. It also offers a decent level of originality, provided you are given clear and specific instructions.

However, the effectiveness of the model is compromised when dealing with highly technical, specialized or highly complex topics. Although ChatGPT has been trained on a wide range of data, its understanding of the material remains superficial. It lacks deep reasoning skills and, therefore, its usefulness in fields requiring a high degree of specialization or analysis may be limited.

Another aspect to consider is the accuracy of the content generated. ChatGPT can make errors of fact or interpretation, so it is imperative that all data be verified and any errors corrected prior to publication.

In addition, the model may have problems maintaining coherence in very long or complicated texts. It may generate content that appears coherent in short segments, but when examining the text as a whole, a lack of thematic or argumentative coherence is observed.

Let's now turn to the ethical and security limitations. ChatGPT can generate text that is politically biased, culturally insensitive or even offensive if restrictions or guidelines are not properly configured. Although the developers have implemented certain safeguards to minimize these risks, the possibility cannot be completely eliminated.

In terms of data security, it is important to remember that most interactions with ChatGPT through online platforms are recorded and stored on servers. While these recordings are primarily used to improve model performance and ensure quality of service, it raises questions about privacy and data ownership.

ChatGPT is a powerful tool for generating textual content, but it is not infallible. Its usefulness varies depending on the type of writing and the objectives you have. The technology is adaptable enough to be useful in a variety of applications, but it has its limitations in terms of accuracy, consistency, and depth of understanding of the material. There are also ethical and safety considerations that should not be overlooked. Knowing these limitations and capabilities will enable you to make more informed and effective use of ChatGPT in your writing project. You will be able to make better decisions about when and how to implement this technology, what editing and revision will be necessary after text generation, and how to handle ethical and privacy issues that may arise.

Chapter 7

Ethical and legal considerations

The integration of artificial intelligence into the field of writing not only opens doors to new opportunities but also raises numerous ethical and legal challenges. This issue is particularly relevant when we are using a technology as powerful as ChatGPT to produce written content that can be monetized and distributed to a wide audience.

Let's start with the question of authorship. When it comes to AI-assisted writing, legitimate questions arise about who actually "owns" the content. Is it the programmer who created the algorithm? The company that owns the model? Or is it the individual who generated the text using the tool? The most likely answer to these questions is that the content generated belongs to the person who instigated it, on the principle that the software is considered a tool in the creative process. However, it is critical to understand the terms of service policies of the AI provider to ensure that no rules regarding intellectual property are being violated.

In addition to intellectual property, there is the question of content originality. Many might argue that the text generated by ChatGPT is simply recycling snippets of information previously trained on the model. Therefore, the quality of "originality" may be a gray area that could pose problems if one attempts, for example, to register the content as an original work.

Another aspect is the veracity and accuracy of the generated content. While language models such as ChatGPT are powerful, they are not infallible and can generate incorrect or misleading information. Depending on the subject matter of the book, the dissemination of false information could have serious ramifications. It is of utmost importance that any content generated is reviewed, corrected and verified by humans to prevent the spread of misinformation.

There are also ethical issues related to data privacy and consent. Although ChatGPT does not store a user's information, the text you generate may be analyzed to improve the performance of the model. Some people might consider this an invasion of their privacy, especially if sensitive topics or confidential information is being discussed.

The issue of bias in algorithms is also another area that deserves attention. All machine learning models, including ChatGPT, are trained on large data sets that reflect the world and, therefore, all of its inherent biases and inequalities. When an author uses ChatGPT to generate content, it is critical to be aware of this fact and review the generated content for any inadvertent biases.

Transparency is another key consideration. While there is no hard and fast rule requiring authors to disclose that they have used AI to generate content, being transparent about this fact could be good practice. This could range from a simple acknowledgement to a more detailed description of how AI was used in the writing process. This transparency can increase reader confidence in the content and at the same time can contribute to a more informed public discussion about the ethical and social implications of AI in creativity. Finally, addressing these ethical and legal issues is not only good from a moral point of view, but could also offer a commercial advantage. Readers and consumers are increasingly informed and value ethics and transparency in the products they consume. Addressing these issues head-on could become a unique selling point that distinguishes your book from others in the marketplace.

Chapter 8

The Science and Art of Prompting

Understanding ChatGPT's Brain:

ChatGPT, at its core, is a marvel of modern technology. But to truly harness its potential, it's essential to grasp the mechanics behind its operations.

Now, I won't bore you with overly technical jargon, but a basic understanding can significantly enhance your interactions.

Imagine ChatGPT as a vast library, with billions of books containing all sorts of information.

But here's the catch: there's no librarian. Instead, you have a guide (the AI) that's read every single book and remembers the content.

When you ask a question or give a prompt, this guide quickly skims through all these books to provide you with the best possible answer based on what it has "read."

Your prompts act as directions for this guide. The clearer and more specific you are, the better the guide can navigate this vast library to fetch the information you seek.

It's not about tricking the AI or using complex language; it's about clarity and precision.

Over the years, I've found that understanding this basic principle can drastically improve the quality of responses from ChatGPT.

It's like having a conversation with a well-read friend; the better your questions, the more insightful their answers.

Crafting Effective Prompts:

The magic of ChatGPT isn't just in its vast knowledge but in its ability to interact in a human-like manner.

However, this magic truly shines when you know how to craft the right prompts. Over time, I've realized that effective prompting is less about asking and more about guiding the AI to the desired response.

Clarity is Key: The first rule of thumb is to be clear in your intent. Ambiguous prompts can lead to equally ambiguous responses.

If you're looking for specific information or a particular type of answer, frame your prompt in a way that leaves little room for misinterpretation.

Context Matters: While ChatGPT is incredibly knowledgeable, it doesn't inherently know the context behind every prompt.

Sometimes, providing a brief background or setting the stage can lead to more accurate and relevant answers.

For instance, instead of asking, "What's its use?", you might say, "In the context of digital marketing, what's the use of SEO?"

Keep it Concise: While it's essential to provide context, there's a fine line between being descriptive and being overly verbose. Aim for conciseness. Get to the point, and avoid unnecessary fluff.

Experiment and Refine: Not every prompt will yield the perfect response on the first try, and that's okay.

Part of mastering ChatGPT is experimenting with different phrasings and approaches. If a response isn't quite what you were hoping for, tweak your prompt and try again.

Use Open-Ended Questions Sparingly: While open-ended questions can lead to insightful answers, they can also yield broad responses.

If you're looking for something specific, try to frame your prompt in a more directed manner.

Over the years, these principles have served as my guiding light in interacting with ChatGPT.

By understanding and applying them, you'll not only get better responses but also develop a deeper appreciation for the art of communication.

Chapter 9

Fundamentals of Natural Language Processing and Chatbots

Welcome to the second chapter of our iBook! In this chapter, we will take an in-depth look at the basics of natural language processing (NLP) and the exciting world of chatbots. Let's dive into the fascinating world of AI and discover how machines can acquire human-like language skills. Language is an amazing faculty of the human mind. We use them to express our thoughts, feelings, and information. Now the question arises: Can we teach machines to understand our language and communicate with us? The answer is yes! And that's what natural language processing is all about.

Natural language processing is an exciting area of artificial intelligence. It enables machines to understand, analyze, generate and respond to human language. This technology plays a crucial role in many areas such as machine translation, speech recognition, sentiment analysis and, of course, chatbots.

Speaking of chatbots - let's go on a fascinating journey through time! We start in the 1960s, when the first chatbot called ELIZA was developed. ELIZA was simple, but she could already have simple dialogues and give human-like answers. Since then, chatbots have continued to evolve and are now more powerful than ever thanks to advances in AI, machine learning, and NLP.

But how do chatbots actually work? How can they understand our language and interact with us? Chatbots use a variety of techniques and algorithms to analyze speech, process queries, and generate appropriate responses. From simple rule-based approaches to complex AI models, there are numerous methods used in the development of chatbots.

The areas of application of chatbots are extremely diverse. They support customer support, help automate workflows, and provide personalized user experiences. In the real estate industry, chatbots can answer customer questions and provide information about available properties. In the IT industry, for example, they provide support in answering technical questions or developing websites. The possibilities are endless!

Of course, there are also challenges in implementing chatbots. Language is complex and ambiguous, and machines must learn to interpret it correctly. Advances in speech recognition, contextual understanding, and NLP models are critical to improving chatbot performance. We will also address ethical issues, privacy and security issues to ensure responsible use of chatbots.

In this chapter we will cover these exciting topics in detail. We will explain how NLP algorithms work, introduce different chatbot models and shed light on practical application examples in various industries. Our goal is to give you a comprehensive understanding of the basics of natural language processing and chatbots and to introduce you to the exciting world of AI.

We are glad that you are part of it and hope that you will be thrilled by this chapter! Let's dive into the fascinating world of natural language processing and chatbots together.

The role of natural language processing in AI:

Natural language processing (NLP) plays an incredibly important role in artificial intelligence (AI). Imagine how amazing it would be if machines could understand our language and communicate with us in a natural way. This is precisely the goal of NLP – it enables computers to understand, analyze, and respond to human language.

NLP is a fascinating field of research that allows machines to understand, interpret, and respond to text or spoken language. Through the use of advanced algorithms and techniques, NLP can analyze complex language structures and grasp the meaning behind the words. This allows machines to understand natural language and interact with us.

The application possibilities of NLP are broad and impressive. One example is machine translation, where NLP models can translate texts or spoken words into another language. This is particularly helpful in a globalized world where communication must take place across language barriers.

Another exciting area of application is speech recognition. NLP models can analyze spoken language and convert it into written text. This allows us to use digital assistants such as Siri or Alexa that can understand our spoken instructions and react accordingly. This makes everyday life easier for us and enables intuitive interaction with our devices.

But NLP doesn't stop there. It plays an important role in sentiment analysis, the recognition and analysis of moods and emotions in texts. Businesses can automatically capture and understand their customers' opinions and reactions through the use of NLP on social media or customer reviews. This allows them to respond appropriately to feedback and sentiment.

In addition, natural language processing forms the foundation for the development of chatbots. By using NLP algorithms coupled with machine learning and artificial intelligence, chatbots can have human-like conversations and respond to questions. They can help us solve problems and support us without us having to deal with complex user interfaces or forms.

The role of NLP in AI is crucial because it allows machines to communicate with us in a way that is familiar and natural to us. This opens up incredible possibilities for the use of AI technologies in our daily lives.

In this chapter, we will take an in-depth look at the basics of natural language processing. We will learn about the underlying techniques and algorithms and explore the wide range of applications in which NLP plays an important role. From machine translation to sentiment analysis and chatbot development, the possibilities are endless and we'll explain everything in an understandable and reader-friendly way.

From ELIZA to Modern Chatbots: A Time Travel

In this chapter, we will embark on an exciting journey through time and explore the history of chatbots. We'll look at the early days of AI research and trace the journey chatbots have taken from the early pioneers to today's sophisticated models.

We start our journey with ELIZA, a groundbreaking chatbot developed in the 1960s. ELIZA was one of the first attempts to get a machine to conduct human-like dialogues. Although it had limited knowledge and was based on simple rule-based patterns, ELIZA was still able to simulate conversations and respond to user input. This was a significant milestone and laid the foundation for the further development of chatbots.

Over the decades, chatbots have evolved and improved. In the 1990s, ALICE and Jabberwacky became known, two chatbots that used machine learning to improve their capabilities. These chatbots have been able to have more natural and realistic conversations because of their ability to learn from previous interactions.

However, the decisive breakthrough came with the advent of machine learning and artificial intelligence in recent years. In particular, the Transformer model, known for its natural language processing capability, has revolutionized the way chatbots work. GPT-3, one of the most advanced transformer models, has shown that chatbots are able to understand complex texts, capture semantic relationships and generate high-quality answers. By training on large data sets, GPT-3 can conduct contextual and nuanced dialogues.

CHAPTER 10

Content Creation Services using CHAT GPT

The 3 best ways to create content using CHAT GPT are:

Blog Post Generation: ChatGPT can efficiently generate blog posts on a wide range of topics. It can provide well-researched and structured articles that can be further customized or edited by content creators. This is especially useful for content marketing and maintaining an active blog.

Product Descriptions and Reviews: ChatGPT can help create product descriptions, reviews, and comparisons for e-commerce websites. It can highlight product features, benefits, and specifications, making it a valuable tool for enhancing product pages.

Social Media Content: ChatGPT can assist in generating engaging and relevant social media content, including captions, tweets, and Facebook posts. It can be used to maintain an active social media presence and connect with the audience effectively.

These three applications leverage ChatGPT's natural language generation capabilities to produce content efficiently and help content creators save time while maintaining content quality.

Blog post generation through ChatGPT is a dynamic and innovative approach that has transformed the landscape of content creation. This technology offers content creators, bloggers, and businesses an efficient and productive means to generate high-quality blog posts on a wide range of topics. Here, we delve into ten essential aspects of blog post generation and its impact on content creation:

Time Efficiency: Blog post generation using ChatGPT significantly reduces the time required for content creation. Instead of starting from scratch, content creators can leverage the AI's capabilities to generate initial drafts, allowing them to focus on editing, refinement, and adding their unique voice to the content.

Content Consistency: Maintaining consistency in writing style, tone, and terminology across a blog is crucial for branding and reader engagement. ChatGPT ensures content consistency by adhering to predefined guidelines and a consistent writing style, reinforcing a brand's identity.

Diverse Content: ChatGPT can produce content on a wide range of topics, making it a versatile tool for bloggers and businesses looking to address various aspects of their niche. This diversity can cater to different audience interests and needs.

Idea Generation: Generating content ideas can be a substantial challenge. ChatGPT can serve as an idea generator, offering a multitude of potential topics, angles, and outlines that can spark creativity and inspire content creators.

Customization: While ChatGPT can generate initial drafts, content creators can customize the content to align with their brand's specific messaging, style, and objectives. This ensures that the generated content remains unique and tailored to their audience.

Keyword Integration: Incorporating relevant keywords is essential for SEO. ChatGPT can seamlessly integrate target keywords into the generated content, enhancing its search engine optimization and visibility on search engine results pages.

Content Updates: As information changes or evolves, content needs to be updated to remain accurate and relevant. ChatGPT can assist in generating new data or insights to be incorporated into existing content, simplifying the process of content refreshes.

Multilingual Content: ChatGPT's multilingual capabilities enable content creation in multiple languages, facilitating global outreach and enabling businesses to connect with a diverse international audience.

Structured Blog Posts: ChatGPT can create well-structured blog posts, including introductions, body content, and conclusions, following the conventional format of a blog article. This ensures that the generated content is organized and reader friendly.

Content Planning: Blog post generation can be incorporated into content planning and editorial calendars. By using ChatGPT to generate drafts in advance, content creators can ensure a steady flow of content for publication, maintain a regular posting schedule, and meet audience expectations.

In summary, blog post generation using ChatGPT is a game-changing tool that empowers content creators and businesses to streamline content creation, improve consistency, and engage with a broader audience. It's a versatile and efficient solution that enhances content marketing strategies and aligns with the demands of the digital age. As this technology continues to advance, it is poised to play an even more significant role in the content creation landscape.

Writing product descriptions and reviews is a critical element in e-commerce and online marketing. It plays a significant role in informing potential customers about a product's features, benefits, and value. Here, we explore ten essential aspects of writing product descriptions and reviews using ChatGPT:

Product Knowledge: Writing accurate product descriptions and reviews requires an in-depth understanding of the product. ChatGPT can assist by providing detailed product information, specifications, and unique selling points, enabling content creators to craft informative and compelling descriptions.

Concise and Engaging Content: Effective product descriptions are concise yet engaging. ChatGPT can generate content that highlights essential information, uses persuasive language, and captures the reader's attention.

Benefits and Features: Product descriptions should clearly communicate the benefits and features of the item. ChatGPT can assist in structuring content that emphasizes what makes the product valuable and how it meets the needs of potential buyers.

Audience Targeting: Content creators can tailor product descriptions to specific target audiences, addressing their unique needs and preferences. ChatGPT can help generate content that resonates with different customer segments.

SEO Optimization: Optimizing product descriptions for search engines is crucial for e-commerce. ChatGPT can suggest and integrate relevant keywords to enhance the product's discoverability in online searches.

Reviews and Ratings: Incorporating customer reviews and ratings into product descriptions can build trust and credibility. ChatGPT can generate review summaries, highlighting the sentiments and feedback of previous customers.

Comparisons and Recommendations: Product descriptions can benefit from comparisons with similar products and recommendations for alternatives. ChatGPT can assist in creating content that helps buyers make informed decisions.

Visual Descriptions: Complementing text-based descriptions with visual content is essential. ChatGPT can provide ideas for image captions and alt text to enhance the overall product presentation.

Customization and Branding: While ChatGPT can generate initial product descriptions, content creators can customize the content to align with their brand's voice and style, ensuring consistency across their product listings.

User Experience: Well-written product descriptions and reviews contribute to a positive user experience. By providing accurate and compelling information, they help potential customers make confident purchasing decisions, reducing the likelihood of returns and improving customer satisfaction.

In conclusion, ChatGPT can be a valuable tool for generating product descriptions and reviews that are informative, engaging, and SEO-friendly. It streamlines the content creation process, empowers content creators to craft compelling narratives around products, and ultimately supports e-commerce success by helping potential buyers make informed decisions. As the e-commerce landscape continues to evolve, the role of AI-driven content generation in product marketing is set to expand even further.

Creating effective social media content is a multifaceted task that requires a deep understanding of your audience, platform-specific dynamics, and the ability to craft engaging and shareable posts. Whether you're a brand looking to connect with your audience or an individual aiming to grow your online presence.

Social media content should be concise, yet impactful. Given the fast-scrolling nature of most social platforms, your message needs to be clear and engaging within a short span of time.

ChatGPT can assist in generating content that is both succinct and attention-grabbing, ensuring that your posts stand out amidst the digital noise.

Tailoring your content to your specific audience is a fundamental aspect of social media success. Knowing your audience's demographics, preferences, and pain points enables you to create content that resonates with them.

ChatGPT can help identify suitable content angles and topics to engage your target audience effectively.

Visual content, including images and videos, is highly shareable on social media. ChatGPT can provide suggestions for captions, descriptions, and hashtags that complement your visual content, making your posts more engaging and discoverable.

Timely and relevant content often garners more attention on social media. ChatGPT can assist in generating real-time content, such as news updates, event coverage, and trending topic discussions, ensuring that your posts remain current and engaging.

Hashtags are essential for content discoverability on platforms like Twitter and Instagram. ChatGPT can suggest relevant hashtags based on the content, helping increase the visibility of your posts to a broader audience.

Engaging with your audience is a crucial part of social media content creation. Responding to comments, questions, and messages in a timely and personalized manner fosters community and loyalty. ChatGPT can provide recommendations for responding to common inquiries and engaging with your followers effectively.

Each social media platform has its unique dynamics and audience behavior. Content that performs well on Facebook might not be as effective on Twitter or Instagram. ChatGPT can generate content tailored to specific platforms, considering character limits, image size requirements, and user expectations.

User-generated content can be a powerful tool for social media engagement. Encouraging your audience to create and share content related to your brand or content is an effective strategy. ChatGPT can assist in generating user-generated content campaign ideas and associated posts.

Content calendars are valuable for consistent posting. ChatGPT can help create a content calendar, suggesting topics, post types, and posting schedules to maintain an active online presence.

Measuring the impact of your social media content is essential. Analyzing engagement metrics, such as likes, shares, comments, and click-through rates, can provide insights into the effectiveness of your content strategy. ChatGPT can guide you on the types of content to focus on based on the performance data.

In summary, writing social media content is a dynamic and strategic endeavor that requires a keen understanding of your audience, platform-specific practices, and engaging content creation. ChatGPT serves as a valuable resource in generating content ideas, suggestions, and strategies to help you create posts that resonate with your audience, promote user engagement, and achieve your social media goals.

CHAPTER 11

UNLEASHING THE POWER OF CHATGPT

Welcome to the gateway of possibilities. In this first chapter, we explore the extraordinary capabilities of ChatGPT, a tool that goes beyond the conventional to become your invaluable companion on the path to wealth. Think of ChatGPT not just as a language model, but as a dynamic force that understands your unique needs and provides tailored insights.

ChatGPT is not an ordinary tool, but your virtual confidant, a sophisticated language model designed to comprehend and respond to your queries with depth. Its vast knowledge base spans a multitude of subjects, making it a treasure trove of information at your fingertips. It's not just a chatbot; it's a conversational wizard, capable of engaging in nuanced discussions and understanding the subtleties of your financial aspirations.

ChatGPT is versatile and adapts to your language, understanding not just what you say, but what you mean. Whether you're a seasoned investor or someone taking their first steps into the world of finance, ChatGPT meets you where you are, breaking down complex concepts into digestible information.

Let's show you how ChatGPT can transform from a mere tool into a catalyst for wealth creation. It's not just about answers; it's about strategic guidance, insights that go beyond the surface, and a roadmap tailored to your unique circumstances.

Think of ChatGPT as your financial guide, navigating the intricate terrain of wealth creation alongside you. Its role is not just to provide information but to empower you with the knowledge and confidence needed to make informed decisions. From investment strategies to understanding market trends, ChatGPT is your reliable companion, ensuring you're equipped with the insights necessary to thrive in the ever-evolving financial landscape.

Consider this chapter as the introduction of a secret partner, the ChatGPT Professor, who stands ready to guide you through the twists and turns of financial exploration. It's not just about accumulating wealth; it's about building a sustainable and meaningful financial future. As we delve deeper into the subsequent chapters, remember that the power of ChatGPT is not just in the information it holds but in the transformation it can bring to your financial journey. Get ready to unleash the full potential of this invaluable tool on your path to wealth!

Chapter 12

The Problem with Prompts

As humans, we desire big results that we can achieve in a short amount of time with minimum effort, this is the appeal of games, TV & social media. There are many adverts and promises made that play on this desire, making us attracted to what they offer. One place this is commonly seen is politics, specifically, political campaigns, where we are told by someone how he/she will provide the result we're looking for, all we need to do is vote for him/her. Another variant of the exploitation of this desire is copy and paste, where we can take something word for word and make little to no changes and just repeat it back, and we'll get the result. A good example of this is the dating field, people are sold promises such as '3 things you can say to any woman to make her instantly like you'. Another is in building relationships, we are told that people like praise and the feeling of importance, to be appreciated, and so when we compliment them, we use general praise words that are flattery, and like before, we're saved from having to do any work, the work, in this case, being thinking more about the other person and their unique personal worth, and complimenting based on that.

This desire for a big result in a short timeframe and with little to no effort is in many cases, as Robert Green called in his book 'The 48 Laws of Power', a fantasy. How to lose ?? Pounds in 30 days with no exercise, make $?? In a week with no experience, 5 steps to happiness, and so on. People make such promises, mostly as adverts for us to give them what they want, usually our money(or a vote), and when we give it to them, they usually don't deliver on the promised result.

Of course not all products, while there are many 'scams', there are others that appeal to us because they do give us the result and greatly reduce the time and effort had we to do it without them. We pay a lot of money, and they deliver, and we are happy. A good example is a car, it saves us a lot of time and energy, and the investment in general is well worth it.

The problem isn't the people and what they promise, as they can be ignored, but our fantasy and desire for 'shortcuts', and not coming to terms with reality, let me explain.

THE REASON & REALITY
What we want is a specific, kind of reality, a desired outcome, to satisfy hunger, to lose weight, to be happy. Whatever it is, it usually requires a series of actions to bring it forth, to

satisfy our hunger, we need to eat, but first the food has to be cooked, and before that harvested, and before that planted. To lose weight usually requires a healthy diet exercise, and so on. These actions are for the most part unavoidable, for they are the means by which the reality we desire comes about. But to take action usually requires effort, many times a lot of it, which we don't like, it's usually painful and we try to avoid it. So when someone makes promises of desired outcomes without the actions, we become very attracted to it. But how can we get the results without action? We can, if someone else does the work for us. Restaurants handle all previous actions in regard to hunger so that all that's left is to order the food and eat. Parents/guardians handle many of the needs of those under them, we want a clean house, so we hire a maid, and so on.

But now when it comes to an outcome such as losing weight or building muscles, no one can do the work of maintaining a healthy diet and exercising for us while we eat junk food & not exercise, it can be made easier, but the action must take place. Many leaders seeking the 'big seat' make promises of how they will make the country a better place if we simply vote for them. But if we take time to look at a country that transformed itself, say China, a huge amount of work needed to be done, something the whole country took part in, and rather than changing leaders who will come with a new set of actions that's unrelated or do away with the actions the previous leader, they pretty much were consistent on the same actions for decades, and the country was truly transformed, when the action was taken. Another example is Amazon, if you are familiar with what Jeff had to do.

The point, whether by force or by choice, someone has to do the work. The education of a child is enormous work, to transform a single individual into not just a functioning member of a society, but one that makes great contributions, is a task very few individuals or organizations can pull off. Most schools can't do that, but a few can, and they are very expensive, cause it's highly valuable. With the right payment, almost any work can be done, think secretaries, projects, financial backing, etc.

This brings us to the second variant of the desire for shortcuts and the one many use AI to exploit, this is when we are told the work is done, so all that's needed is to copy & paste/rinse & repeat. The problem with this, especially when it comes to dealing with humans, is that the effort required is putting thought into it, but when given copy & paste, it becomes thoughtless and loses its deeper meaning. To put it another way, it doesn't tap into the unique wants and needs of the other. I think women can relate to this when someone tries to woo them with pick-up lines they've heard before. But when it comes to relationships, I want to believe we've all in one way or the other experienced when we were genuinely appreciated vs when we were flattered. In the former, something we identify with and make us feel a sense of self-worth, but not recognized immediately is as Vanessa Van puts it, 'Highlighted', we feel more self-confident and happier about ourselves, we appreciate that it was recognized, and pointed out. But in the latter, it's so dull, hardly giving any effect, we know the person feels he should just say something good, especially when it's followed by criticism. Sometimes it might even be annoying, and we generally don't care about it; 'Oh you're so smart', 'Good work', and so on (Just remembering some as I write this makes me think; "Yeah whatever, you don't have to pretend like you care"). Notice what happens is that no work/effort is put in to think about the other person or their unique qualities. It's usually insincere because the person does not care, or at least didn't show signs of it. In a way, he still tried to avoid the work needed, and while outward it sounded like the former, still identified as praise, the meaning, which is where the value is, is missing. Think about this, cause you'll notice this with ChatGPT also, i.e. marketed as the action is done, all you need to do is copy & paste, rinse and repeat.

Needless to say, tech plays into this, with the many apps or software that promise to get the job done, people usually fall into the trap of moving from one gadget/software to the other, rather than getting any work done. It's all the same appeal of getting the result without you having to do the work, which won't be a problem if the issues mentioned above are addressed.

Now ChatGPT is the technology of today with this promise, and while a good deal of the work is done, more work still needs to be done to get to the desired outcome. Think of a car, it saves time and energy, but people don't buy cars for the sake of driving, they buy among other things- to get from place to place, so you still need to go there (or get a driver). Similarly, you don't use ChatGPT just to chat with it, you need answers or tasks accomplished for you.

In short, to achieve our goals, we take action. And some of these actions, the value is not on the surface like cleaning and cooking, the value is in the meaning behind them, which requires effort. When these two are addressed, then we are able to achieve our goals. This is the issue with a good deal of the prompts that are ready-made for us to copy and paste, they are not tapping into specific needs and desires thus having no meaning, but it doesn't have to be so. ChatGPT can be used effectively in a way that allows us to achieve our goals.

This book you're reading is an example, clearly, it's not AI written, but AI did help, as a compliment, not lead. I can tell it what to write, but it won't write this. One is because am human, but two, I have real-world experience, I understand that there are a lot of promises about ChatGPT, and people want to know how they can use it to the best of its capabilities. I am aware of what they need to achieve what they want, and as I write, I draw from other experiences I believe are relevant to what am discussing and include them. Am not just spouting random words for the sake of writing, but am being creative, in a way that's unique to me and solves reader's problems. Now that I've explained the importance of effort taken, thoughts and actions to achieve what we want, let's now look at how to actually use ChatGPT to get those results we want.

Chapter 13

The Business of Chat GPT

ChatGPT is a powerful tool for creating high-quality content, but it can also be a powerful tool for building a successful business. In this chapter, we'll discuss how to monetize AI-generated content, how to use advertising and sponsorships to generate revenue, and how to build a sustainable business model with ChatGPT.

Monetizing AI-generated Content

One of the most obvious ways to monetize AI-generated content is through advertising. By creating high-quality content with ChatGPT, you can attract a large audience, which can be valuable to businesses looking to advertise their products or services. Advertising can be done through platforms such as Google AdSense, which allows you to include ads on your website, or through platforms like YouTube, which allows you to include ads in your videos.

Another way to monetize AI-generated content is through sponsorships. This can be done by reaching out to businesses in your niche and pitching them your content. You can also use platforms like TikTok, which has a Creator Fund program, to monetize your content.

In addition to advertising and sponsorships, you can monetize AI-generated content through affiliate marketing. This is when you promote a product or service on your website or social media platforms and earn a commission for every sale made through your unique affiliate link.

Advertising and Sponsorships

Advertising and sponsorships are two of the most common ways to monetize AI-generated content. Advertising is when a business pays you to include their product or service in your content.

Sponsorships are when a business pays you to

create content that promotes their product or service.

To monetize your content through advertising, you can use platforms like Google AdSense, which allows you to include ads on your website, or platforms like YouTube, which allows you to include ads in your videos. To monetize your content through sponsorships, you can reach out to businesses in your niche and pitch them your content.

Building a Sustainable Business Model with ChatGPT

To build a sustainable business model with ChatGPT, it's important to focus on creating high-quality content that will attract and retain a large audience. Additionally, it's important to monetize that content through advertising, sponsorships, and affiliate marketing.

It's also important to diversify your revenue streams. This can be done by offering services such as content creation, scriptwriting, and social media management to businesses in your niche. Additionally, you can create and sell digital products such as e-books and online courses that teach others how to use ChatGPT to create high-quality content.

Another way to build a sustainable business model with ChatGPT is to develop and sell a software or application that utilizes the power of ChatGPT. This can be done by developing a chatbot that utilizes ChatGPT's natural language processing capabilities, or by creating a content generation tool that utilizes ChatGPT's ability to generate high-quality text.

In conclusion, ChatGPT is a powerful tool for creating high-quality content, but it can also be a powerful tool for building a successful business. By monetizing AI-generated content through advertising, sponsorships, and affiliate marketing, and building a sustainable business model with

ChatGPT, you can generate significant revenue. However, it's important to keep in mind that ChatGPT is a tool, and a human touch is always needed to make a business truly successful.

Chapter 14

The Ethical Considerations of ChatGPT

As with any technology, there are ethical considerations that must be taken into account when using ChatGPT. In this chapter, we will discuss some of the ethical considerations of ChatGPT, including bias and accountability in AI-generated content, transparency and regulation, and mitigating negative consequences.

Bias and Accountability in AI-generated Content

One of the most significant ethical considerations of ChatGPT is bias. Because the model is trained on a dataset of text, it can inadvertently learn and replicate biases that exist in the data. This can lead to the generation of content that is discriminatory or offensive. Additionally, because ChatGPT generates text autonomously, it can be difficult to hold anyone accountable for the content it produces.

To mitigate these issues, it's important to ensure that the dataset used to train the model is diverse and free of biases. Additionally, it's important to regularly monitor and review the content generated by ChatGPT to ensure that it is free of discriminatory or offensive language.

Transparency and Regulation

Another ethical consideration of ChatGPT is transparency and regulation. Because ChatGPT is an AI model, it can be difficult for users to understand how it works and how it generates text. Additionally, because ChatGPT is capable of generating highly realistic and convincing text, it can be used to spread misinformation or propaganda.

To mitigate these issues, it's important for companies and organizations that use ChatGPT to be transparent about how the model works and how it generates text. Additionally, it's important for governments and regulatory bodies to establish guidelines and regulations for the use of AI-generated content, particularly in terms of transparency and accountability. This can include guidelines for labeling AI-generated content, as well as regulations for companies and organizations that use ChatGPT to ensure that they are held accountable for any negative consequences that may arise from the use of the model.

Mitigating Negative Consequences

Another ethical consideration of ChatGPT is the potential for negative consequences. As the model is capable of generating highly realistic and convincing text, it can be used to spread misinformation, engage in cyberbullying, or even manipulate people.

To mitigate these negative consequences, it's important to use ChatGPT responsibly and with a clear understanding of its capabilities and limitations. Additionally, it's important to have a plan in place to address any negative consequences that may arise from the use of the model. This can include having a team in place to monitor and review AI-generated content, as well as guidelines and protocols for addressing any negative consequences that may arise.

In conclusion, ChatGPT is a powerful tool for generating text, but it's important to use it responsibly and with a clear understanding of its capabilities and limitations. By being aware of the ethical considerations of ChatGPT, such as bias and accountability in AI-generated content, transparency and regulation, and mitigating negative consequences, we can ensure that the technology is used ethically and for the benefit of society.

Chapter 15

The Digital Goldmine: Understanding ChatGPT's Earning Potential

In the ever-evolving digital landscape, new frontiers of income generation emerge, shifting how we perceive and acquire wealth.

One such paradigm shift is the advent of ChatGPT, a platform that converges technology and human ingenuity, allowing for a unique income-generating experience.

ChatGPT isn't merely a tech novelty; it's a digital goldmine, a testament to the innovative spirit of the online world.

It harnesses the power of conversational AI, enabling individuals like you to earn income through meaningful interactions.

This isn't about passive income; it's active, engaging, and requires creativity, empathy, and strategic thinking.

But how does one navigate this promising yet intricate space? How can you, regardless of your technical background, maximize this opportunity?

This chapter serves as your comprehensive guide, your first step into ChatGPT.

We won't dangle promises or vague possibilities in front of you. Instead, we offer concrete information, grounded insights, and actionable steps.

You'll learn the mechanics of how ChatGPT functions as an income source, dissecting its monetization model to understand where the earning potential lies.

We'll unveil the strategies employed by successful ChatGPT earners, providing you with practical examples to emulate.

Moreover, we'll guide you through the initial setup, ensuring you're well-prepared to embark on this journey.

The digital realm is abundant with opportunities, but it favors the informed and the proactive. So, as we delve into the world of ChatGPT, remember: the knowledge you acquire is valuable only when it's applied.

This isn't just a learning endeavor; it's a call to action, an invitation to participate in a digital revolution that's redefining the very concepts of work, income, and financial independence.

Introduction to ChatGPT: The Frontier of Earning in the Digital Age

At the heart of the digital earning revolution is ChatGPT, a platform that uniquely combines artificial intelligence with human interaction, creating a space where communication translates into income.

But what exactly is ChatGPT, and how does it fit into the broader picture of online earning opportunities?

Understanding ChatGPT:

ChatGPT stands at the intersection of technology and human creativity. It's a platform that allows users to engage with an AI in meaningful exchanges, with the twist of monetization added to the mix.

Unlike traditional online tasks that might involve repetitive activities with little room for creativity, ChatGPT thrives on your unique human input. Your responses, conversation handling, and ability to engage with users are what drive your earning potential.

The Rise of Conversational AI Platforms:

The concept might seem futuristic, but it's a natural progression in the age of AI. As businesses and consumers alike have grown more comfortable with AI interactions (think virtual assistants, chatbots, and recommendation algorithms), the demand for more sophisticated, human-like exchanges has skyrocketed.

ChatGPT is part of this wave, bridging the gap between AI's capabilities and the human touch that makes interactions valuable and relatable.

Why It Matters for Online Income Seekers:

For those looking to earn money online, ChatGPT represents a significant opportunity. It's not about exploiting a system but about contributing to the AI's learning, making it more effective, and providing value to end-users. In return, you receive compensation for your input and engagement.

It's a merit-based system where your effort and skill directly influence your earnings.

The Democratization of Earning Opportunities: Perhaps most notably, ChatGPT democratizes the earning landscape. You don't need specialized technical knowledge, and there's no gatekeeping based on formal education or background.

All that's required is your ability to communicate effectively, respond with empathy and creativity, and commit to consistent participation on the platform.

Direct Application:
To get started, your first step is straightforward: sign up on the ChatGPT platform. The process is simple, requiring basic information and acceptance of the platform's guidelines.

Once registered, familiarize yourself with the user interface, understand the types of prompts you may encounter, and start engaging. Remember, each interaction is a chance to improve, learn, and increase your earning potential.

Monetizing Conversations: *Turning Dialogue into Dollars*

Navigating the ChatGPT platform for profit isn't about chance; it's about strategy. Understanding the monetization model is crucial, as it influences every interaction you have on the platform.

Here, we dissect the components of earning through ChatGPT, offering you a clear roadmap to financial gain through your dialogues.

Understanding the Earning Mechanics:

ChatGPT operates on a pay-per-interaction model. Each conversation you engage in contributes to your earnings, but not all interactions are valued equally.

The platform assesses the quality of your responses, measuring factors like engagement, relevance, and user satisfaction. It means you earn more from interactions that provide value to the end-users, encouraging quality over quantity.

Strategies for Quality Interactions:

Engagement is Key: Users come to ChatGPT for engaging, human-like interactions. Your ability to keep the conversation flowing, interesting, and on-topic is crucial.

Practice active listening techniques, even in this digital format. Pay attention to user prompts, respond with thoughtfulness, and avoid generic replies.

Personalization Matters: Avoid cookie-cutter responses. Tailor your replies to each user, considering their unique inquiries, tone, and conversation style.

Personalization enhances user satisfaction, potentially increasing your earnings for each interaction.

Stay Informed and Versatile: The more topics you can competently discuss, the better your earning potential. Stay informed about popular subjects, current events, and general knowledge.

Versatility increases your chances of engaging more users, as your conversations aren't limited by topic expertise.

Maximizing Earning Opportunities:

ChatGPT offers various tiers of earning potential, often based on user ratings and consistent performance. To maximize your earnings, maintain a high level of quality in your interactions.

Here's how:

Seek Continuous Improvement: Use the feedback provided by ChatGPT and its users to refine your approach. Constructive criticism is an opportunity for growth, directly impacting your earning potential.

Consistency and Volume: While quality trumps quantity, volume still matters. The more high-quality interactions you have, the more you earn.

Set dedicated time daily to engage on the platform, ensuring you meet volume targets without compromising interaction quality.

Understand the Rating System: ChatGPT users can rate their interactions, which influences your visibility and earning potential on the platform. Strive for positive ratings by providing value-driven, enjoyable conversations.

Direct Application:
Start by analyzing your current interactions on ChatGPT. Are there common themes in the feedback or ratings? Identify areas for improvement and implement changes in your next set of interactions.

Monitor the changes in your performance metrics and earnings. Remember, improvement is an ongoing process, directly linked to your earning trajectory on the platform.

Success Stories: **Learning from ChatGPT Champions**

While the mechanics of earning through ChatGPT are straightforward in theory, real-world examples provide the most compelling evidence of what's truly possible.

In this section, we spotlight individuals who have carved a niche for themselves on ChatGPT, turning strategy into success. These stories serve not just as inspiration but as blueprints to emulate in your journey.

From Casual Chatter to Earning Champion: *Jake's Story*

Jake, a college student studying linguistics, stumbled upon ChatGPT during its early days. Initially, he treated it as a novel way to pass time, engaging in conversations spanning various topics.

However, he soon noticed that his background in linguistics gave him an edge in crafting compelling, engaging narratives with the users.

Recognizing the potential, Jake began to dedicate more time and strategy to his interactions.

He stayed abreast of trending topics, tailored his responses to user behavior, and consistently sought feedback for improvement.

His efforts paid off as he saw his earnings on the platform multiply, providing him not just with extra income, but valuable communication experience.

Key Takeaways from Jake:
Leverage your unique skills or background to enhance your interactions.
Stay informed and adaptable to user preferences.
Treat feedback as a tool for growth and refinement.

Full-Time Income on a Flexible Schedule: *Linda's Journey*

For Linda, a stay-at-home parent, ChatGPT was a gateway to earning without compromising her family commitments.

She found that the platform's flexibility allowed her to work around her schedule, logging in during her free hours and engaging with users from all walks of life.

What set Linda apart was her strategy. She focused on empathetic engagement, often providing a listening ear to users who needed to vent, discuss personal dilemmas, or seek unbiased opinions.

Her empathetic approach resonated with users, earning her high ratings and consistent positive feedback, which in turn increased her visibility and earning potential on the platform.

Key Takeaways from Linda:
Empathy is a powerful tool in human-centric services like ChatGPT.
The platform's flexibility supports various lifestyles and commitments.

Positive user experiences are crucial for visibility and higher earnings.

Direct Application:
Reflect on your unique circumstances, skills, or experiences. How can you apply these to your interactions on ChatGPT?

Consider the strategies employed by Jake and Linda.

Are there elements you can adapt to fit your style or situation?

Implement these strategies in your next interactions and observe any shifts in user engagement or feedback.

Setting Up for Success: Your Starter Pack for ChatGPT

Embarking on your ChatGPT journey is more than signing up and diving into conversations.

It requires a strategic setup to ensure your efforts are directed efficiently from the very beginning. This section is your starter pack, guiding you through the initial steps necessary to position yourself for success on the platform.

Seamless Sign-Up

Your first interaction with ChatGPT is the sign-up process, and it's as straightforward as it gets.

You'll need to provide some basic information, agree to the platform's terms of service, and confirm that you understand the guidelines and policies. Ensure you read these thoroughly, as they outline what's expected of you and what you can expect from ChatGPT.

Optimizing Your Profile

While ChatGPT doesn't function like social media, your profile matters. It's not about profile pictures or catchy bios; it's about setting your preferences, areas of interest, and expertise.

This information helps the platform direct suitable conversations your way, aligning with your strengths and knowledge areas.

Navigating the Dashboard

Familiarity with your ChatGPT dashboard is crucial. It's your command center, where you'll access conversations, track your earnings, receive feedback, and find valuable resources.

Spend time understanding the different functionalities, settings, and metrics displayed. Knowing where to find what you need saves time and keeps you focused on your interactions.

Engaging with the Community

ChatGPT boasts a vibrant community of users, and engaging with this network can be incredibly beneficial. You'll find forums, discussion groups, and resource hubs where users share tips, experiences, and updates.
 Participating in these communities not only enhances your knowledge but also keeps you informed of any platform changes that could affect your strategy.

Setting Realistic Goals

Before you dive into conversations, set clear, realistic goals for your ChatGPT journey. Are you aiming for a specific earning target? Do you want to dedicate a set number of hours per week? Having clear objectives allows you to track your progress, stay motivated, and adjust your strategies as needed.

Direct Application:

Begin with the end in mind. As you complete your sign-up, take the time to navigate through the platform thoroughly.

Join community discussions, set your initial goals, and engage in a few conversations to get a feel for the process.

Remember, every successful journey begins with well-thought-out first steps.

Your dedication to understanding and optimizing your initial interaction with ChatGPT lays the groundwork for the success to come.

Chapter 16

The ChatGPT Revolution: Your Key to Unlocking a World of Opportunities

Understanding ChatGPT: A Game-Changer in the Tech Industry

Welcome to the first subchapter of your life-changing journey! Here, we will begin by diving deep into the world of ChatGPT, understanding what it is, and exploring why it's considered a game-changer in the tech industry. By the end of this subchapter, you'll have a solid foundation of knowledge about ChatGPT and be eager to learn how to harness its power to generate income and achieve financial success.

So, what is ChatGPT? ChatGPT is an AI language model developed by OpenAI, based on the GPT-4 architecture. This groundbreaking AI technology has the ability to understand and generate human-like text, making it an incredibly powerful tool for a variety of applications. From content creation to customer service, ChatGPT has taken the tech industry by storm, revolutionizing the way we work and communicate.

But why is ChatGPT considered a game-changer? To understand this, let's take a look at some of the key features that set ChatGPT apart from other AI models and make it an invaluable resource for those looking to generate income and change their lives.

Human-like Text Generation: One of the most impressive aspects of ChatGPT is its ability to generate human-like text. This means that the content it creates is not only coherent and engaging but also virtually indistinguishable from something a human writer might produce. This level of quality is invaluable when it comes to creating content that resonates with readers and drives results.

Customizable and Versatile: ChatGPT is highly customizable, allowing users to tailor its output to meet their specific needs. By providing it with a prompt or set of instructions, users can guide the AI to generate content that aligns with their desired tone, style, and format. This versatility makes ChatGPT suitable for a wide range of applications, from blog posts and social media updates to sales copy and email campaigns.

Time and Cost Efficiency: Creating high-quality content can be time-consuming and expensive, particularly for those without a background in writing or marketing. ChatGPT offers a solution to this problem by generating top-notch content quickly and efficiently, saving users time and money. This efficiency is particularly valuable for those looking to generate income, as it allows them to focus on other aspects of their business and scale their operations more effectively.

Accessibility for Non-Tech-Savvy Users: While some AI technologies can be complex and difficult to navigate, ChatGPT has been designed with user-friendliness in mind. Its intuitive interface makes it accessible to individuals with little or no technical expertise, allowing them to harness its power to create content, streamline their workflow, and ultimately, generate income.

Now that you have a better understanding of what ChatGPT is and why it's considered a game-changer, you may be wondering how it can help you generate income and achieve financial success. The answer lies in its ability to create high-quality content that engages readers and drives results. By leveraging ChatGPT's capabilities, you can tap into the growing demand for AI-generated content and build a thriving business that caters to this market.

In the upcoming subchapters, we'll explore how to get started with ChatGPT and utilize its features to create content that resonates with your target audience. We'll also discuss the importance of using ChatGPT ethically and responsibly, ensuring that your content remains authentic and transparent.

So, are you ready to embrace the power of ChatGPT and take your first steps towards financial success? Let's continue on this exciting journey together, unlocking the secrets of ChatGPT mastery and transforming your life for the better.

As we dive deeper into the world of ChatGPT, it's essential to understand the growing demand for AI-generated content and the potential it presents for those seeking financial success. The digital landscape is constantly evolving, and businesses and individuals alike are seeking innovative ways to stand out from the competition and connect with their target audience. AI-generated content, particularly that produced by ChatGPT, offers a solution to this challenge, enabling users to create engaging, high-quality content at scale.

This growing demand for AI-generated content has created a wealth of opportunities for those who can master ChatGPT and use it to their advantage. By tapping into this market, you can build a thriving business or side hustle, offering content creation services to clients and generating passive income through various monetization strategies. Moreover, as the popularity of AI-generated content continues to rise, the potential for growth and success in this field is virtually limitless.

One of the key factors driving the demand for ChatGPT-generated content is its ability to save businesses and individuals time and money. High-quality content creation can be a significant investment, particularly for smaller businesses or entrepreneurs with limited resources. By utilizing ChatGPT, they can access top-notch content at a fraction of the cost, enabling them to allocate their resources more effectively and focus on other aspects of their business.

Another driving factor is the need for constant content in today's digital age. With the ever-increasing number of platforms and channels available for content distribution, businesses and individuals are under constant pressure to produce fresh, engaging content that captures their audience's attention. ChatGPT offers a solution to this challenge, enabling users to create a wide range of content quickly and efficiently.

As the demand for AI-generated content continues to grow, so too does the potential for those who can harness the power of ChatGPT to generate income and achieve financial success. By mastering ChatGPT and offering content creation services to clients, you can tap into this lucrative market and build a thriving business or side hustle.

However, with great power comes great responsibility. As a ChatGPT expert, it's crucial to use the platform ethically and responsibly, ensuring that your content remains authentic, transparent, and compliant with any applicable laws and regulations. In the upcoming subchapters, we'll delve deeper into the importance of ethical AI use and discuss how to create content that aligns with your values and those of your target audience.

In conclusion, understanding ChatGPT and its role as a game-changer in the tech industry is the first step towards unlocking its potential for financial success. By embracing its capabilities and tapping into the growing demand for AI-generated content, you can create a thriving business that caters to this market and ultimately transform your life for the better.

So, buckle up and get ready for an exciting journey as we explore the ins and outs of ChatGPT, helping you master this groundbreaking technology and use it to change your life. With determination, perseverance, and the right guidance, you'll soon be on your way to achieving financial success through ChatGPT.

Chapter 17

Getting Started with ChatGPT: The Life-Changing Opportunity You Can't Miss

Are you ready to embark on a life-changing journey that will take your income generation to new heights? In this subchapter, we'll guide you step by step through the process of getting started with ChatGPT. As you follow along, you'll quickly realize that this groundbreaking tool is the opportunity you've been waiting for – one that you simply can't afford to miss.

First, let's address the question on everyone's mind: Why is ChatGPT such a fantastic opportunity for making money, particularly for non-tech-savvy individuals? The answer lies in its accessibility and versatility. With its user-friendly interface and powerful text-generation capabilities, ChatGPT levels the playing field, allowing anyone – regardless of their technical background – to create high-quality content and tap into the lucrative market for AI-generated content.

Now, let's dive into the process of getting started with ChatGPT. Follow these simple steps, and you'll be on your way to mastering ChatGPT and generating income in no time:

Sign up for an OpenAI account: To access ChatGPT, you'll need to create an account with OpenAI, the company that developed this revolutionary technology. The sign-up process is quick and straightforward, and it will provide you with access to the tools and resources you need to start using ChatGPT.

Familiarize yourself with the ChatGPT interface: Once you've signed up for an OpenAI account, take some time to explore the ChatGPT interface and familiarize yourself with its features. This will help you feel more comfortable and confident using the platform, which is essential for maximizing your success.

Experiment with prompts and instructions: One of the keys to mastering ChatGPT is learning how to provide it with the right prompts and instructions. Spend some time experimenting with different prompts and instructions to see how the AI responds. This will help you understand how to guide ChatGPT to generate the content you desire.

Refine your writing style: As you experiment with ChatGPT, you'll discover that it's capable of generating content in a wide range of styles and tones. Take some time to refine your writing style and find the right voice for your content. This will help you create content that resonates with your target audience and drives results.

Understand your target market: To generate income with ChatGPT, you'll need to understand your target market and the types of content they're looking for. Spend some time researching your niche, analyzing your competition, and identifying content gaps and opportunities. This will help you create content that stands out and attracts clients.

Imagine being able to generate a steady stream of income by creating high-quality content for clients or monetizing your own content. That's the power of ChatGPT. It's an opportunity that can change your life, and it's one that you can't afford to pass up.

As you continue on this journey, you'll discover countless ways to leverage ChatGPT's capabilities to generate income and achieve financial success. From offering content creation services to clients to creating and monetizing your own digital products, the possibilities are endless. And the best part? You don't need any technical expertise to take advantage of this incredible opportunity.

So, don't wait any longer. Seize this life-changing opportunity and start mastering ChatGPT today. The financial success you've been dreaming of is within reach, and all it takes is a little determination, persistence, and the guidance provided in this book. Before you know it, you'll be on your way to transforming your life and achieving the financial freedom you've always wanted.

In the following subchapters, we'll dive deeper into the various methods and strategies you can use to generate income with ChatGPT. We'll discuss content creation services, digital product creation, passive income generation, and more. By the time you've finished this book, you'll have a comprehensive understanding of how to leverage ChatGPT to change your life for the better.

But before we dive into those exciting topics, let's pause for a moment and consider the possibilities that lie ahead. Imagine being able to create top-notch content for clients in record time, freeing up your schedule and allowing you to pursue your passions. Picture yourself creating and selling digital products that generate passive income while you sleep, providing you with the financial freedom to live life on your terms.

Sound too good to be true? It's not – and ChatGPT is the key that unlocks the door to these incredible opportunities. With ChatGPT, you can create content that rivals that of professional writers, providing you with a competitive edge in the marketplace. And because ChatGPT is so easy to use, even those with no technical skills can quickly become proficient and start generating income.

If you're still on the fence about the potential of ChatGPT, consider this: According to a recent study, the global AI-generated content market is expected to reach $21.2 billion by 2028. That's a staggering growth rate that underscores the increasing demand for AI-generated content across industries. By mastering ChatGPT, you'll be positioning yourself at the forefront of this booming market, setting yourself up for long-term success.

Moreover, as you become more skilled at using ChatGPT, you'll discover that it's not just a tool for generating content – it's a platform that fosters creativity, innovation, and personal growth. By working with ChatGPT, you'll hone your writing skills, deepen your understanding of your target audience, and develop a keen sense of the type of content that drives results. In short, mastering ChatGPT will not only help you generate income – it will also help you grow as a content creator and entrepreneur.

Still not convinced? Let me share a story that might change your mind. Sarah, a stay-at-home mom with no technical background, stumbled upon ChatGPT while searching for ways to supplement her family's income. Despite her lack of experience, she decided to give it a try, and she quickly discovered that ChatGPT was the answer she'd been looking for.

By mastering ChatGPT, Sarah was able to build a thriving content creation business from scratch, providing her with a steady stream of income and the flexibility to spend more time with her family. Today, Sarah is not only financially secure – she's also happier and more fulfilled than she's ever been. And it all started with ChatGPT.

So, are you ready to take the plunge and start your journey towards financial success with ChatGPT? With determination, persistence, and the guidance provided in this book, there's no limit to what you can achieve. As we move forward into the following subchapters, we'll explore the various methods and strategies you can use to generate income with ChatGPT, providing you with the tools and knowledge you need to change your life for the better. Don't wait any longer – your future success is just around the corner.

Content Creation Services: Your Ticket to a Lucrative Career

Are you ready to discover one of the most effective and lucrative ways to generate income with ChatGPT? In this subchapter, we'll explore the exciting world of content creation services – a booming market that offers you a golden opportunity to make money while doing what you love. We'll discuss how to leverage ChatGPT's powerful capabilities to create high-quality content for clients, as well as tips and strategies to help you succeed in this competitive field. First, let's talk about why content creation services are such a hot commodity. In today's digital age, businesses and entrepreneurs are constantly searching for fresh, engaging content to help them stand out in a crowded online marketplace. High-quality content is essential for attracting new customers, building brand awareness, and driving sales. And that's where ChatGPT comes in.

With ChatGPT, you can quickly and easily create top-notch content that meets the needs of your clients – and you can do it without breaking a sweat. This means you can offer your services to a wide range of clients, from small businesses to large corporations, and generate a steady stream of income while enjoying the flexibility and freedom that comes with being your own boss.

So, how do you get started in the world of content creation services using ChatGPT? Here are a few essential steps to help you hit the ground running:

Identify your niche: To succeed in the content creation business, it's crucial to focus on a specific niche or industry. By specializing in a particular area, you'll be able to develop a deep understanding of your target market's needs and preferences, allowing you to create content that truly resonates with your audience. Spend some time researching different niches, analyzing your competition, and identifying areas where your skills and interests align.

Create a portfolio: Before you can start offering your services, you'll need to showcase your skills and expertise. Develop a portfolio of content samples that demonstrate your ability to create high-quality content using ChatGPT. This will help potential clients understand the value you can bring to their projects and give them confidence in your abilities.

Set your rates: Determine how much you'll charge for your content creation services. Consider factors such as the time and effort involved in creating the content, as well as the value you're providing to your clients. Be sure to research the going rates for content creation services in your niche, so you can price your services competitively.

Market your services: Now that you've identified your niche, created a portfolio, and set your rates, it's time to start marketing your services. Use social media, online forums, and networking events to connect with potential clients and showcase your expertise. Be proactive in reaching out to potential clients, and don't be afraid to share your success stories and testimonials from satisfied customers.

As you begin to attract clients and build a reputation for creating top-notch content, you'll find that the demand for your services continues to grow. This is your chance to establish yourself as a sought-after content creator, generating a steady stream of income and achieving the financial success you've always dreamed of. But the benefits of offering content creation services using ChatGPT don't stop there. By mastering ChatGPT and developing your skills as a content creator, you'll also be investing in your own personal and professional growth. As you work with clients and create content for a variety of industries, you'll gain valuable insights and experiences that will help you become an even better content creator and entrepreneur.

So, are you ready to take the plunge and start your journey towards financial success with content creation services and ChatGPT? The opportunity is there for the taking – all you need is the determination, persistence, and guidance provided in this book. As we continue to explore the various methods and strategies for generating income with ChatGPT, you'll be equipped with the tools and knowledge you need to change your life for the better. Remember, success is within your reach – it's up to you to seize it.

In the upcoming subchapters, we'll delve deeper into other exciting ways to make money using ChatGPT, including digital product creation, passive income generation, and more. Each method will offer its own unique advantages and opportunities, allowing you to choose the path that best suits your skills, interests, and goals.

As you read and learn, don't forget to apply the concepts and strategies discussed in this book to your own journey towards financial success with ChatGPT. Take the time to practice your skills, refine your strategies, and learn from your experiences. As you do, you'll find that the possibilities for making money with ChatGPT are virtually endless – and you'll be well on your way to creating a life that's not only financially secure but also deeply fulfilling.

So, buckle up and get ready for an exciting adventure. Together, we'll unlock the secrets of ChatGPT and discover the incredible potential it holds for transforming your life and achieving your dreams. With each step you take and each subchapter you read, you'll be one step closer to the financial success you've always desired.

In the next subchapter, we'll dive into the world of digital product creation using ChatGPT – a powerful method for generating income that allows you to leverage your creativity and expertise. We'll discuss how to create and sell digital products that captivate your audience, generate passive income, and help you achieve financial freedom. Don't miss out on this amazing opportunity – continue reading, and let's embark on this life-changing journey together.

So, you might be wondering, what makes content creation services such an incredible opportunity for making money using ChatGPT? Let's take a closer look at some of the key benefits and examples that illustrate the true potential of this income-generating method:

Low startup costs: Unlike many other businesses, starting a content creation service using ChatGPT requires minimal upfront investment. All you need is a computer, an internet connection, and a subscription to ChatGPT. This makes it an accessible option for individuals from all walks of life, no matter their financial situation.

Flexibility: One of the biggest advantages of offering content creation services is the flexibility it provides. You can work from anywhere, at any time, and set your own schedule. This allows you to strike a balance between work and personal life, reducing stress and increasing overall job satisfaction.

Scalability: As your content creation business grows, you can easily scale your operations by outsourcing work to other ChatGPT users or hiring a team to help you manage the increased workload. This means that the sky's the limit when it comes to your earning potential.

Diverse clientele: With ChatGPT, you can cater to a wide range of clients, from small business owners to large corporations, and even individual entrepreneurs. This diversity ensures that you'll never run out of potential clients to work with and that your services will always be in demand.

Let's explore a real-life example that demonstrates the potential of content creation services using ChatGPT. Meet John, a college student who was struggling to make ends meet while pursuing his degree. Frustrated with his part-time job's low pay and inflexible hours, John decided to give ChatGPT a try.

John quickly discovered that he had a knack for using ChatGPT to create engaging content, and he began offering his services to local businesses in his community. Word of John's exceptional work spread, and before long, he was juggling multiple clients and generating a steady income.

With ChatGPT's help, John was able to pay off his student loans, cover his living expenses, and even save for the future – all while maintaining a flexible schedule that allowed him to focus on his studies. Today, John's content creation business continues to thrive, providing him with the financial stability and freedom he once only dreamed of.

John's story is just one example of the life-changing impact that offering content creation services using ChatGPT can have. As you embark on your own journey, remember that success is within your reach – all it takes is determination, persistence, and the willingness to learn and grow.

So, why wait any longer? The world of content creation services using ChatGPT is an open book, just waiting for you to write your own success story. With each step you take and each new skill you learn, you'll be one step closer to achieving the financial success and freedom you've always desired. Embrace the journey, and let ChatGPT be your guide to a brighter, more fulfilling future.

As we dive deeper into the world of content creation services, it's essential to understand the different types of content that you can create using ChatGPT, as well as how to tailor your offerings to different client personas. By doing so, you'll be able to maximize your income potential and provide a truly valuable service to your clients.

Let's take a closer look at John's story and the types of content he offered, as well as some other content options that you might consider for your own content creation business.

John initially started by offering blog posts and articles for local businesses in his college town. He focused on small businesses, such as restaurants, boutique shops, and fitness studios. These businesses were looking to build their online presence and drive traffic to their websites through engaging, informative content.

To make his services appealing to these businesses, John priced his blog posts and articles at $50 for a 500-word piece. As his reputation grew and he gained more experience, John was able to increase his rates to $75 per 500-word article.

John's primary target persona was the local small business owner – someone who was passionate about their business but lacked the time or expertise to create their own content. By offering a valuable service that met their specific needs, John was able to forge strong relationships with his clients and generate a steady stream of income.

As John's content creation business expanded, he began to explore other types of content that he could create using ChatGPT. Some of these content options include:

Social media posts: Creating engaging, shareable content for platforms like Facebook, Twitter, and Instagram can be a highly lucrative service to offer. Many businesses struggle to maintain a consistent presence on social media, and providing a steady stream of high-quality posts can help them attract new followers and increase brand awareness.

Email newsletters: Email marketing is still one of the most effective ways for businesses to communicate with their customers and drive sales. Crafting compelling newsletters that showcase a company's products, services, or industry news can help businesses retain existing customers and attract new ones.

Web copy: Writing persuasive, compelling copy for websites is an essential skill for any content creator. By offering web copy services, you can help businesses improve their online presence, optimize their websites for search engines, and convert visitors into customers.

E-books and guides: Creating informative, value-packed e-books and guides can help businesses establish themselves as experts in their industry and generate leads. By offering e-book and guide creation services, you can tap into a growing market for digital products and generate passive income through sales or royalties.

By exploring these various content options and tailoring your services to meet the needs of different client personas, you'll be able to diversify your income streams and build a more sustainable content creation business.

Remember, the key to success in the content creation industry is to understand the unique needs and preferences of your target audience and to provide a valuable, customized service that meets those needs. By doing so, you'll not only generate income but also build a reputation for excellence – just like John did.

Now that you have a better understanding of the different types of content and client personas, you're well on your way to building a successful content creation business using ChatGPT. Keep refining your skills, expanding your service offerings, and pursuing new opportunities – and watch as your financial success grows along with your expertise.

www.ingramcontent.com/pod-product-compliance
Lightning Source LLC
LaVergne TN
LVHW010222070526
838199LV00062B/4688